PALMISTRY

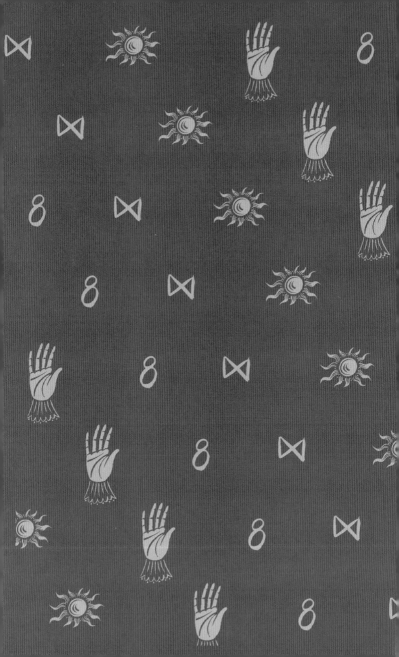

PALMISTRY

ROMAYNE MARJOLIN & HANNAH REINER

ELEMENT

Shaftesbury, Dorset • Rockport, Massachusetts • Melbourne, Victoria

© Element Books Limited 1997

First published in Great Britain by
ELEMENT BOOKS LIMITED
Shaftesbury, Dorset SP7 8BP

Published in the USA in 1997 by
ELEMENT BOOKS INC.
PO Box 830, Rockport, MA 01966

Published in Australia in 1997 by
ELEMENT BOOKS LIMITED
and distributed by Penguin Australia Ltd
487 Maroondah Highway, Ringwood, Victoria 3134

Designed and created with
THE BRIDGEWATER BOOK COMPANY

Printed and bound in Singapore

British Library Cataloguing in Publication data available

Library of Congress Cataloging in Publication data available

ISBN: 1 86204 131 8

ELEMENT BOOKS LIMITED
Editorial Director *Julia McCutchen*
Managing Editor *Caro Ness*
Project Editor *Allie West*
Production Director *Roger Lane*
Production *Sarah Golden*

THE BRIDGEWATER BOOK COMPANY
Art Director *Peter Bridgewater*
Designer *Stephen Minns*
Managing Editor *Anne Townley*
Project Editor *Caroline Earle*
Picture Research *Julia Hanson*

Endpapers *Sarah Young*
Illustrations *Ivan Hissey and Paul Collicutt*
Model maker *Mark Jamieson*
Studio photography *Guy Ryecart*
Endpapers *Sarah Young*

Picture Credits:
e.t. archive: 11 (Pietro de Muttoni: The Palm Reader. Civic Museum, Vicenza).
Hutchison Library: Tony Souter, front cover, 7. The Image Bank: © Game, 12.
Images Colour Library: 1, 13, 23, 30, 54, 55. Rex Features: 50. Werner Forman
Archive: Field Museum of Natural History, Chicago, front cover, 4. Zefa Colour
Library: front cover, 5, 10, 39, 48 (B), 49.

CONTENTS

INTRODUCTION

The art of palmistry is a technique which has been practiced for many thousands of years. By studying the shape of the hand and the many lines etched into the skin, a palmist can judge our personal character and predict our destiny.

WHAT IS PALMISTRY?

The art of palmistry requires the subtle fusion of two ancient disciplines; cheirognomy – the study of the nature of hands, and how their shape and marking, texture and color, relate to character – and cheiromancy – the divination of life events from the hand.

Like all enduring means of divination, palmistry is a tool with which to observe our personalities and to judge which of our characteristics will have the most impact on our lives. For this reason,

A NATIVE AMERICAN SYMBOL OF MAN'S AGE-OLD BELIEF THAT HANDS GIVE INSIGHT INTO THE FUTURE.

the art of palmistry can be used to foretell the future for a limited time and in a limited way.

The practice of palmistry does, however, require experience and intelligence. Character cannot be analyzed by glancing, for instance, at the "heart line." A short heart line does not necessarily mean a non-existent love-life. For one thing, the hand markings are just a small part of the picture; for another, the hand changes over time. Hand-reading is not a matter of making judgments, but of identifying trends.

If you set out to advise yourself or others through the insights you may gain from these pages, you are taking on a responsibility. Take palmistry seriously and you will be rewarded with a heightened awareness of character, the wisdom to rejoice in strengths, and the ability to identify weaknesses. You will learn how to focus on the positive aspects of life and act in good time to avoid pitfalls.

THE HISTORY OF PALMISTRY

God sealeth up the hand of every man; that all men may know his work.

JOB 37:7

ANCIENT CULTURES BELIEVED THAT THE HAND REVEALED A PERSON'S FATE.

Palmistry was practiced in China and India at least 3,000 years ago, with ancient texts alluding to the telling of a person's fate from the shape, lines, and patterns on their hand. In China it was, and is still, part of a larger attempt to study destiny by scrutinizing the face, hands, and forehead in order to identify a person's "correct path." In India palmistry is linked to astrology.

In Ancient Greece palmistry was known as chirosophy (from *xier*, hand,

and *sophia*, wisdom). The Greek philosopher, Aristotle, wrote of the great interest people had in their hands, and the existence of those specially skilled in reading the palm for the purpose of learning the future.

In the early Christian era, a papal edict of 315 C.E. decreed that anyone who practiced palmistry "outside the Church" could be excommunicated or put to death. By the Middle Ages, the Church still saw palmistry as a threat, even though it was mentioned in the Jewish *Zohar*.

In England, during the reign of Henry VIII (*1509–1547*), its practice was still severely punished; as late as the reign of George IV (*1820–30*), palmistry was banned by law.

> *"Any person found practicing palmistry is hereby deemed a rogue and a vagabond, to be sentenced to one year's imprisonment, and to stand in the pillory."*

ACT OF PARLIAMENT

INTERPRETATIONS

Each age re-interprets palmistry in the light of its own knowledge – and for that reason, the various terms given to parts of the hand can be studied and read, just like fossil layers in rock.

We find the names of ancient gods attributed to the digits and fleshy mounds of the hand. Echoes of astrological and numerological mysteries are present too: parts of the hand are said to be ruled by the seven traditional planets (*see pages 40–5*), while the number five has a rather obvious significance.

In the Middle Ages, hand-reading was governed by the four elements of earth, air, fire, and water. Qualities, such as melancholic, sanguine, choleric, and phlegmatic, were attributed to them.

In Victorian England, it was fashionable to see character – particularly criminal tendencies – indelibly marked in the shape of the head, the physiognomy, and by extension, the hand. Rigid lists were created to label the individual types, and hands were systematically classified into seven categories by the palm-reader D'Arpentigny, author of *Chirognomie, le science de la main*, published in England in 1886.

Count Louis Hamon (*1866–1930*), known as "Cheiro," whose influence extended well into the 20th century, pursued the belief that palmistry was a science that had serious implications. His credibility was somewhat damaged by statements such as "it has been recently proved that gray matter similar to that of the brain can be found in the tips of the fingers of blind persons."

In this century, the respected psychoanalyst Carl Jung (*1875–1961*) was fascinated by the findings of a palmist called Julius Spier, who wrote *Psychochirology*, published in England in 1944. Jungians believe – reflecting Jung's theories of extraversion and intraversion – that the outward personality is in the right hand while the inner, secret one is in the left. This view marked the

A GYPSY PALMISTRY CHART SHOWS
SOME OF THE INFLUENCES BELIEVED TO
RULE DIFFERENT PARTS OF THE HAND.

return to a much more traditional interpretation of palmistry after the rigid pseudo-science of Cheiro and the Victorians.

In Britain, the art of hand-reading may have existed since the time of the Druids, who used a form of communication called "Finger Ogam." This was based on the phalanges, palm, and movements of the hand, that were used to communicate with one another in complete secrecy.

PALMISTRY TODAY

Today, we see fine lines on the hand as energy paths and the hand itself as a type of personal computer, recording events in our lives. We have learned how markings increase on, or near, Apollo or Fate lines at certain points (*see pages 32–3*); and we believe that our hands alter, not necessarily every seven years – as the ancients thought – but according to events in our lives.

✯

SETTING THE SCENE

✯

It is essential that there is trust between the palmist and the subject. A palm-reading should take place in a quiet room, where the light is good, so that you can see clearly. Daylight is best, as electric light may alter the appearance of skin tones.

CONDITIONS FOR A READING

The successful practice of palmistry requires sympathy between the palmist and the subject. A palm-reading should take place in a quiet room, in a relaxed atmosphere, enhanced, if you wish, by calming, scented oils.

A certain amount of preparation will take place before the final reading. Hands should be clean, and free of nail polish or false nails. There should be access to soap and water, and the materials for taking a palmprint (*see page 10*).

The initial discussion should put the subject at ease. This discourse gives the palmist an opportunity to discover which is the dominant hand (if the person is right-handed, it is the right hand) and to prepare to take the palmprint. The palmist should also notice gesture and body language. The open and expansive, or closed and defensive, or flamboyant attitudes in which the hands are held in relation to the body, are crucial to an understanding of the whole personality.

- *Look at and palpate (examine with your hands) the whole hand. Notice texture, color, blemishes, fingernails, and the presence of rings.*
- *Ask the person to wash and dry their hands and remove any rings.*
- *Take a palmprint from the dominant hand: palmprints enable the hand to be seen fully.*

- Ask the subject to wash and dry their hands a second time.
- You should then read the palmprint alongside both hands.
- File the palmprint with your notes.

THE DOMINANT HAND

The theory of opposites – of balance between opposing forces – is central to reading character and destiny. Like the "yin" and "yang" of Eastern philosophy, these opposing forces are not "good" and "evil" but positive and negative, and complement one another. Without perfect balance, there is disharmony.

The dominant hand represents all that is conscious, open, and active. It reflects events as they are. The minor hand represents contemplation and discretion, privacy and dreams; it portrays potential.

A reading of an individual's dominant hand will reflect what is actually happening, and has happened, in the person's life. This includes achievements

BALANCE, AS EXPRESSED IN THIS YIN & YANG SYMBOL, IS THE KEY TO PALMISTRY.

and disappointments, changing views, and the outward expression of the kind of person they are. The hand's three major lines (heart, head, and life) represent the physical organs of the body.

On the minor hand, inner desires and aspirations are marked. A fascinating insight into the person's true potential can be seen on this hand. In the three major lines on the minor hand there is a picture of the deep, nervous, emotional, and sexual energy that is driven by the personality.

INTERPRETING THE WHOLE HAND

First you will learn to assess the shape of the hand, according to D'Arpentigny's classifications – in other words, square, spatulate, or other shape (see pages 12 – 17). You will then learn to judge the relative balance between the two sides of the hand – the coolness or clamminess of skin texture, and the pink or yellow tone of the skin. Look for anything out of the

The dominant hand reflects events as they are

The min hand re aspiratic

A PALMIST ASSESSES AND
INTERPRETS EVERY DETAIL AND
VARIATION OF A SUBJECT'S PALMS.

ordinary. Exaggerated features may be balanced in some other part of the hand, and you must be able to observe everything, weighing characteristics as part of the overall balance.

Significant differences evident between the two hands, may explain difficulties; perhaps indicating that two sides of the individual's personality are in conflict.

Hands unusually criss-crossed with lines indicate highly strung emotions, while very "empty" hands belong to calm people (although they may go to pieces in a crisis). The flesh of the palm should be firm, indicating self-reliance.

You will draw fulfillment from palmistry in such measure as you practice it. At first, you will be surprised by the variety of hands that you see, and you will be daunted by the factors that must be taken into account. But as the years pass, you will find yourself humbled and fascinated by an art about which there is always more to learn.

TAKING A PALMPRINT

 It's impossible to give a correct reading of the hand (remember it is the dominant hand on which you will base your reading) without first taking a palmprint.

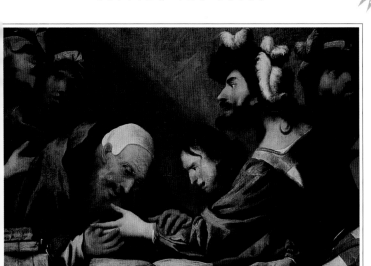

PIETRO DE MUTTONI'S *THE PALM*.
A PALMIST BASES A READING ON ONE
HAND, THE DOMINANT ONE.

The reason for this will be apparent as soon as the impression appears on the paper, for much more shows up on paper than it is possible to see on the palm itself.

The true characteristics of the major lines, complete with stars, squares, triangles, and many other symbols, become apparent as soon as you take an impression.

The usual method of taking an impression is to roll printing ink from a ceramic tile onto the hand using an old rolling pin, and then to press the hand onto paper. Peel the hand from the paper to reveal a clear palmprint beneath. If you can't obtain the right kind of ink, shoe polish, makeup, or various kinds of paint may be appropriate – an office ink-pad works well. Whatever you choose, the medium should not be so oily or wet that lines are smeared. Above all it should be washable; experiment, if you wish, on your own hands.

THE HANDS

Palmistry involves reading the whole hand, not just the palm. The 19th-century French palmist, D'Arpentigny, classified hand shapes into the groups that we recognize today. To judge the shape of a hand, you first have to understand what long or short, wide, or narrow means.

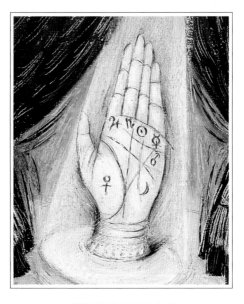

ASSESS THE WHOLE HAND TO
DETERMINE ITS CLASSIFICATION.

THE HANDS

Palmistry encompasses far more than just the lines and bumps of the palm. Assessment of the whole hand is crucial; most hands can be classified according to the shapes listed by D'Arpentigny over a hundred years ago.

HOW TO MEASURE AND CLASSIFY

To judge the shape of the hands you have to learn to under-stand the variations in shape and size, and decide what long or short, wide or narrow, means in that context. When you have assessed lots of hands you will see the indi-vidual features of a person's hands at once, but until then you need a scale with which to measure. Start by turning the hands palm-side up and look at the width and length of the palms. If they are the same, the palm is square. If the hands are longer than they are wide, they are considered to be rectangular.

Next, measure the fingers. Take the longest one – almost always the middle finger – and bend it towards the wrist. If it doesn't reach the base of the wrist, the fingers are consid-ered to be short. If it just reaches the base of the palm, they are of normal length, and if it touches the wrist easily, then the person has long fingers.

Bearing these assessments in mind, classify the hand according to type. It may be square – for instance, square-palmed with short fingers. It may be excessively square – known as elementary – that is a noticeably wide, short hand with a short thumb.

The conic hand has a long rectangular palm and rounded fingertips; in its extreme it is psychic, with slim fingers and a straight thin thumb. Spatulate hands are either narrow at the base of the palm and wider at the finger ends, or narrowing into a bunch at the finger ends but wide at the base. The philosophic hand is longish and bony.

The radial area is the thumb side of the hand and the ulna the opposite side. If the radial has strong firm fingers with unusually high mounds on the radial palm, there will be dynamism in active, worldly matters. If the ulna is more pronounced, the person will be a home-lover who is creative and good at self-expression.

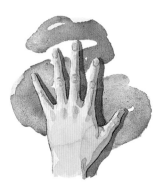

A SPIRIT OF ADVENTURE IS AMONG THE CHARACTERISTICS OF SOMEONE WITH A SPATULATE HAND.

SPATULATE HANDS

 Those with a purely spatulate hand are independent, energetic, and original. They are ambitious, impatient, and like to be asked to come up with ideas. There is an inventiveness, an ability to make discoveries that partly stems from their original view of the world. They are entrepreneurial, willing to take risks, and exciting company. If there's a chance to go cross-country skiing, or to make a parachute jump, this person will be the one to seize the opportunity. However, be careful; in their restlessness they may take short cuts, be slapdash, or bend the rules further than seems prudent.

SQUARE AND ELEMENTARY HANDS

 The square hand, that measures about the same at the wrist as it does at the base of the fingers, belongs to a person who is practical and rational. You can always rely on those with square hands to do exactly what they have promised to do, on time. They are doggedly persistent and sometimes very successful. No breath of scandal will ever touch them and if it did, they would fight to the bitter end to clear their name.

A SQUARE HAND SUGGESTS A PRACTICAL, RELIABLE, AND PERSEVERING NATURE.

There can be something in the purely square-handed person which is maddeningly conventional, predictable, and may occasionally verge on the humorless.

The pure elementary hand, a sub-genre of the square, is the one the Victorian palmists most feared to see. With their fixed ideas about criminality being inborn and demonstrated by physical characteristics, they were convinced that the possessor of the "elementary hand" was a potential Lizzie Borden or Bonnie or Clyde.

This was, of course, inaccurate. The elementary hand, with its fingers shorter than the palm, its very short thumb, and few lines, indicates a person who finds it hard to communicate. This may resolve itself into happiness in some pedestrian, practical employment. The only temptation to violence in this person stems from a frustrated desire for self-expression.

A CONIC HAND SUGGESTS OPTIMISM, GENEROSITY, AND SENSUALITY.

CONIC HANDS

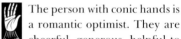 The person with conic hands is a romantic optimist. They are cheerful, generous, helpful to their friends, and always ready with a constructive plan for getting the best out of any situation. They are sensual and impulsive.

Perhaps, because of their trusting good nature, they are sometimes disillusioned, and tend to lose their capacity to judge people at all, becoming oversensitive to slights from those who mean no harm. This may make them unduly cautious and reactive in relationships. They are the kind of people who make excellent friends, though if you meet them late in their life it may take some time to get to know them.

COMMUNICATION IS NOT A STRENGTH OF SOMEONE WITH AN ELEMENTARY HAND.

A PSYCHIC HAND IS INDICATIVE
OF A TRUSTING NATURE.

As a result of their unrealisti
expectations they are destine
always to suffer disappointment
on a personal, as well as a politica
level. In later life these disappoint
ments may make them becom
reserved or even embittered wit
their lot.

THE INTELLECTUAL MAY HAVE LONG,
PHILOSOPHIC HANDS.

PSYCHIC HANDS

 The psychic hand is the graceful conic hand in its exaggerated form, with pointed, tapering fingers, and a long palm. This person is sweetly sensitive, compassionate, and trusting; too much so, sometimes, for their own good. Life is often painful to them. The person with psychic hands weeps for disasters they are at a loss to prevent, adopts every lame duck they come across, and gives their heart once only, usually to a person who will almost certainly fail to live up to such an overwhelming and self-denying passion.

PHILOSOPHIC HANDS

Long, bony hands are calle
"philosophic." They belong t
an intellectual who appear
impractical and easily distracte
from the minutiae of life. Althoug

heir chaotic surroundings make hem seem eccentric, paradoxically t is their very practicality that tells hem not to bother with minor, ime-consuming matters when there are big problems to be solved. They ee the wider picture, and in some enses are more practical than those who have their noses to the grindtone and their feet on the ground.

In their greatest incarnations, hey may be actively philanthropic and capable of moving the hearts and minds of many. However, they are impatient with the more prosaic needs of others and are inclined to gnore their feelings.

MIXED HANDS

Many hands, as you will find when you have examined ten or twelve sets in detail, are mixed n some way. This is where your skill s tested, because you have to weigh he relative importance of their various features against each other. There are also some types that ranscend D'Arpentigny's classifications, such as the claw-like hand, hat gives a rather rapacious impression, and the hand with the hollow palm. Such features may be found n hands of any type.

MANY PEOPLE ACTUALLY POSSESS MIXED HANDS.

A claw-like hand, so long as it is free from arthritis, may be a sign of long-term anxiety over money or the future in general; the hollow palm usually belongs to a timid or cautious person.

Every feature should be weighed in balance with others on the same hand, and then compared with those on the minor hand.

SKIN TEXTURE

Most of us have, at some time or other, received an unpleasantly damp handshake. This clamminess is common and will be apparent when palpating. You should never remark upon it.

CLAMMY? DRY SKIN? A HANDSHAKE TELLS
YOU MUCH ABOUT SOMEONE'S PERSONALITY.

Notice, though, the firmness or flabbiness of the hand, any heightened blue or red tones, any unusual prominence, flexibility, or stiffness. The lines on the hand should be slightly darker than the skin around them; undue whiteness may be a sign of poor health; a bluish tinge may indicate anemia.

Heat and cold, clamminess and dryness, helped the medieval philosophers to classify hands according to personality type. Serious, melancholy, earth people had warm, dry hands; cool air people were airy and sanguine about life; fiery, hot-handed types were choleric; and the clammy water people were non-communicative and phlegmatic. You may find that although these typologies appear superficial, they are in fact surprisingly accurate.

THE THUMB

The first thing to notice about the thumb is how it is naturally held. If it's curled defensively within the palm this is usually a sign of insecurity.

Its size should be proportionate to the rest of the hand. To determine its relative length, place the lowest knuckle of the thumb on the dominant hand, on the percussion line below Mercury (the little finger) or the minor hand. The thumb and Mercury should be the same length.

The thumb represents will-power, and the clear-sightedness that should develop with time.

Strong thumbs show a capacity to deal with life; the owner of long thumbs is rational, a leader, and a clear thinker. People who have short thumbs may, given the wrong circumstances and no overriding characteristics, become subordinate and unhappy, for in their confusion they lack the will to resist stronger characters. A stubby thumb means aggression and a tendency to abuse power. A person who has waisted thumbs (*see page 48*) will doubt their own instincts, and will always look for ulterior motives in others.

ANGLE AND SETTING OF THE THUMB

 Ask the subject to hold out their hand, with the thumbs and fingers apart. If the thumb lies closer to the index finger at an angle less than 45 degrees, the person has an overcontrolled nature. A 90-degree angle between thumb and forefinger signifies an outgoing, charming, and extrovert personality.

When you look at the back of the hand as it is lying flat on the table, you will see that the thumb opposes the fingers (the thumbnail at right angles) or aligns with them (thumb-nail and fingernails facing in roughly the same direction). Direct opposition is often seen where a person bottles up resentment and has a tendency to become embittered. The thumb that is open, however, may mean generosity to the point of over-indulgence – even with oneself.

To define the setting of the thumb, divide the hand mentally into quadrants. Draw an imaginary line between the middle and ring fingers, and a line across that at the mid-point. If the thumb is set well below that line, the person will be lively, resolute, and clear about the material things she wants from life. The high-set thumb belongs to a person who is creative, but perhaps irresolute, something of a dreamer who lets opportunities pass by and cares little about making a living.

PHALANGES OF THE THUMB

 The thumb's two phalanges (sections) represent will (the top one) and logic (the lower), and they should be about the same length. An imbalance is significant. If the lower phalange is longer than the upper, this is someone who thinks and probably talks a lot, but doesn't get much done; a dominant upper phalange, on the other hand, indicates a person who rushes into things and then demands help when they get into hot water.

A flattened thumb-pad can be a sign of low self-esteem, sometimes emerging as promiscuous behavior. The general outline of the thumb-tip is echoed in the fingers, with the square tip indicating practicality, a conic tip signifying idealism, and a well-shaped spatulate thumb showing manual dexterity.

FINGER LENGTH

 The fingers are as important to hand-reading as the lines on the palm. Their names are:

⑥ *Jupiter, the index finger*

⑥ *Saturn, the middle finger*

⑥ *Apollo, the ring finger*

⑥ *Mercury, the little finger*

Measure the fingers from the palm side, taking the angle of slope into

---

> ⑥ *An upper phalange bent back at the top is the "spendthrift's thumb" though this is often negated by other signs on the hand.*
>
> ⑥ *A jutting thumb tends to mean stubbornness, and the stubby, clubbed thumb always indicates strong will.*

account, and notice which finger dominates. They should be seen in relation to each other. As the radius (*see page 13*) represents the conscious, outgoing side, and the ulna (*see page 13*), the inner, unconscious side, the middle fingers should provide balance and control. Weak middle fingers indicate a lack of control.

DOMINANT FINGERS

 The pure Jupiterian has a longer Jupiter finger than Apollo, and a well-developed mound (pad on the palm) beneath the Jupiter finger. This is an ego-driven character, for good or ill; a leader, sometimes a religious leader or a soldier.

The pure Saturn type has a long Saturn finger flanked by Jupiter and Apollo of equal length. This

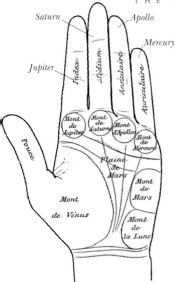

Saturn
Apollo
Mercury
Jupiter

THE LENGTH OF THE FINGERS AND
THEIR RELATIONSHIPS TO EACH OTHER
ALL GIVE CLUES TO CHARACTER.

The pure Mercurian type, whose little finger rises well up above the top joint of Apollo, is someone who is likely to be endowed with quick-silver intelligence, shrewdness in business affairs, and with a charismatic personality.

FINGERTIPS

 The possessor of conical or pointed fingertips is artistically inclined. Remember that truly pointed fingers are the extreme of this type, and may veer toward irrationality or oversensitivity.

A pointed Jupiter finger often belongs to a hermit or religious person, who is out of touch with everyday life. The pointed Saturn finger also tends to indicate a certain lack of practicality, while the pointed Apollo may belong to someone so avant-garde that they are competely out of touch with reality.

Square or spatulate (square but slightly waisted) fingertips denote a rational, practical person, although a person with square tips is the extreme – they may be down to earth to the point of finding new ideas difficult. Spatulate fingertips are the ideal, showing both enthusiasm and confidence.

personality is serious and controlled, and their curiosity is well developed. Saturnians make good mining engineers, code-breakers, or researchers; they are diggers.

The pure Apollonian has a longer Apollo finger than that of Jupiter, and is emotional and intuitive – one who basks in feelings. This person makes a good healer or counselor. However, a short Apollo finger can signify dependence, emotional immaturity, or even an unjustified belief in one's own talent.

PHALANGES

 The phalanges (the sections between the finger-joints) are read from the top down. The first phalange represents introspection and concern, and the second corresponds to one's attitude to the material world.

A long, firm second phalange on the Apollo finger is a sign of an agent or dealer who can market artistic work.

However, any indications from the first and second phalanges can be outweighed by the third phalanges if they are too heavy; the third phalanges represent the earthiest of physical desires.

SETTING AND ANGLE OF THE FINGERS

 Middle fingers leaning towards the radius show an over-awareness of appearances. This person is repressed in public, but can compartmentalize their life and show quite a different face to their friends. Middle fingers leaning outwards to the ulna show that repressions are very deep. Though the personality may seem shallow or show-stoppingly open, fun to be

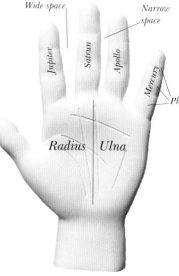

THE SIZE OF GAP BETWEEN THE FINGERS CAN ALSO SUGGEST PERSONALITY AND CHARACTER TRAITS.

with, and unafraid to communicate on every level, one must not be deceived; there may be dark secrets and even turmoil in the heart.

Apollo leaning towards Saturn indicates emotional confusion hiding behind outward reasonableness, a fear of the emotions, and to some extent a tendency to manipulate others. Mercury hiding behind Saturn indicates an unwillingness to communicate through reticence, shyness, and lack of confidence.

SETTING AND GAPS BETWEEN FINGERS

Notice the way the fingers are normally set along a line that slopes gently towards the ulna. If this is completely straight, that is, horizontal rather than sloping, the person may be charmlessly selfish. If, on the other hand, there is a dramatic plunge from Jupiter to Mercury, there may be over-dominant parents and a feeling of inadequacy. If both Jupiter and Mercury are set low, there will be a need for affection.

The gaps between the fingers are of great significance too. A wide space on the active, outgoing radial side between Jupiter and Saturn indicates confidence and self-sufficiency; a narrow space shows a need to do the conventional thing. This gap is concerned with relationships with the world at large.

If the space between Saturn and Apollo is narrow, it may demonstrate a conflict between family and career, or opposition between the individual's practical need to survive and their artistic integrity.

The person whose Mercury (communication) finger leans away from the others, has a deep need to be alone. If Mercury and Apollo are close together, there will be difficulty in personal relationships.

The gestural language of the hands is crucial. If all the fingers are held together during an argument, there is an unwillingness to be contradicted or interrupted, while if they are left open and evenly spaced, there is a willingness to take new views on board.

Remember the old warning about a person with gaps between their fingers when the hand is closed; these are said to be gaps through which money can slip!

JOINTS

The first joint of the finger (the one at the top) represents mental order, and the second, material order. If both are prominent, the person will be over-controlled. If only one is prominent, expect a dominance by the mental or material side of the character within the sphere relevant to the finger – Jupiter, the ego; Saturn, the researcher; Apollo, the artist; Mercury, the communicator. Thorough, analytical types tend to have prominent joints on all their fingers, while intuitive people are smooth-fingered. Some palmists believe that knobbly joints show a blockage of psychic energy within that sphere; thus, for instance, a knobbly upper joint on Mercury could be an indication of a frustrated desire to communicate.

FINGERNAILS

 Measure fingernails from the base to just below the white tip. Long nails are longer than they are wide, and short nails are wider than they are long. Other nails are likely to be more or less square, rounded, or fan-shaped.

The possessor of very long nails will internalize problems and perhaps release resentment as sarcasm. They may be prone to chest disorders. The short-nailed person is far more likely to make a fuss, in fact to be almost belligerent, while fan-shaped nails show nervousness.

Nails should be smooth, healthy, and pink with visible moons. These kinds of nails indicate not only good health, but also an open and frank nature. Small moons are a sign of low blood pressure and, possibly, poor circulation.

Unusually, small nails show a delicate constitution and perhaps a certain languor. If the nails are brittle, pale, or flecked with white spots, then the person's general health may not be good. Curved, bulbous, or blue nails may indicate a cardiac problem.

A person with wide, short nails has lots of energy, quick reactions, and is sexually aggressive and possessive. If the nails are longer, the person is more cautious, sensible, and reserved.

Wide, round nails are a sign of placidity and dreaminess, while someone with very shallow nails is usually a complainer. Watch out for the person with long, deep-set nails who can be selfish, though is clever enough to disguise it.

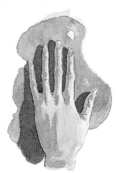

SOMEONE WITH LONG NAILS IS LIKELY TO BE CONTROLLED OR EVEN BOTTLED UP.

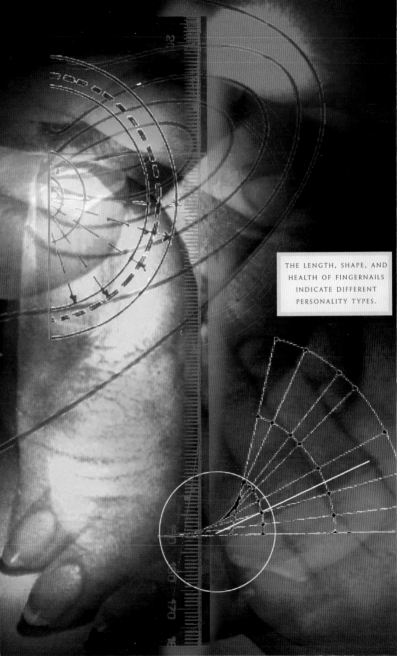

THE LENGTH, SHAPE, AND
HEALTH OF FINGERNAILS
INDICATE DIFFERENT
PERSONALITY TYPES.

SKIN RIDGE PATTERNS

 The examination of tiny marks on the hand is called "dermatoglyphics," and close study of these patterns is perhaps the most revelatory aspect of hand-reading.

A whorl is a definite, positive sign, although like all other indicators it has a less attractive side – in this case a tendency to be rigid.

Where the peacock's eye (an elongated whorl inside a loop) is seen, there will be protection against accident or ill-fortune.

A whorl or loop on the mound of Luna, the mound low on the ulna side (*see page 45*), is a sign of psychic ability and the determination to pursue it.

A whorl on Saturn shows that this person is brave enough to think and act independently, even when others disagree.

A loop usually heightens the positive aspects of the sphere in which it is found. For example, between Jupiter and Saturn, it indicates leadership and authority; between Saturn and Apollo, it shows the capacity to achieve through effort; if it is found between Apollo and Mercury, there will be a love of good company anda sense of humor. A loop right across Apollo, however, can unbalance this sphere and tend toward vanity.

The arch is an active, well-meaning, constructive sign. It is a great adviser, and, on Saturn or Apollo especially, shows the ability to file, document, and keep practical records. This is the sign of the busy organizer. However, a tented (squeezed) arch may signify a need to be pushed into doing things.

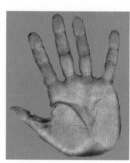

BRAVERY, A SENSE OF HUMOR, OR CLERICAL SKILLS CAN BE DISCERNED FROM TINY MARKS ON THE HAND.

WHEN IN A GROUP OF
PEOPLE, SEE IF YOU CAN
OBSERVE WHAT THEIR
HANDS TELL YOU
ABOUT THEM.

✦

PROMINENT LINES

✦

The prominent lines of the hands are the features amateur palmists pore over at garden parties, but they can only be read effectively in conjunction with other signs. They are just one of the visible sets of markings, bumps, and shapes that, taken together, indicate character and destiny.

MAIN LINES

There are a number of markings visible on the palms of your hands, but the four most important lines are the life, head, heart, and fate lines.

THE LIFE LINE

The person with a long and well-marked life line will generally have a healthy, happy life, although length alone is no firm indicator of longevity (many centenarians have short life lines). Signs worthy of note are vertical or horizontal lines leaving or crossing it, as well as marks and hooks.

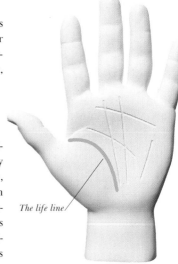

The life line

The life line should always be read from the top, near Jupiter, downward as it skirts the mound of Venus toward the wrist.

Small upward branches toward Jupiter mean ambition. However, if there is a sharp line falling from the top of the life line, inside it, there may have been a sudden loss or change of circumstances during childhood.

Upward hooks appearing along the life line indicate achievement; appearing after some indicator of misfortune, they may indicate that there was a huge effort to struggle out of adversity at that particular time.

The person whose life line clings to Venus, circling the base, will stay near home most of their life, while the one whose life line trails toward the ulna side may live abroad; there is a certain restlessness here. The life line that swoops down dramatically close to the thumb, shows a certain lack of vitality.

Splits along the line indicate evolutionary change, maybe even some kind of conflict between domestic life and outside interests, but more often a life change caused by moving house or taking up a new job or relationship.

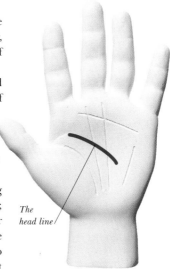

The head line

THE HEAD LINE

The head line should be firm and well-marked like the life line, without noticeable chaining. It runs, generally, at a gentle slant across the hand, commencing on the radial side below Jupiter. This slant shows intuition and imagination, although if it descends at an unusually precipitous angle it should ideally be tempered with practicality in other areas. Where there is no slope at all, and the head line is straight, sympathy and imagination are lacking.

MANY TEXTS THROUGHOUT THE AGES REFER TO
PALMISTRY. THE FAMOUS OCCULT TEXT *LUDICRUM
CHRIOMANTICUM PRAETORIS* FEATURES
PALMISTRY SCENES.

Head and life lines should begin separately, showing a willingness to be independent of one's family in fact and in opinion. Slavishly obedient or dependent people tend to have head and life lines that are tied at the start.

Upward branches from the head line are signs of success in the spheres they point toward; to Jupiter for leadership, Saturn for research and hard work, Apollo for the arts and entertainment, and Mercury for communication or business. The head line with a branch down to the mound of Luna (on the ulna side opposite the thumb) means academic achievement in the arts or humanities.

If the head line runs right across the hand, terminating on the mound of Upper Mars and in the middle of the ulna side, this person could be very bright but egotistical. Should a head line terminate at Mercury, there will be success in business, often at the expense of other people.

Small branches downward anywhere along the head line, indicate periods of slight depression.

THE HEART LINE (AND THE SIMIAN LINE)

The heart line, which reveals relationships, not only of a romantic nature, is rarely simple and straight. In fact, an abnormally straight line would be a sign of cold rationality toward other people. This person would be unwilling to give anything at all. However, the steeply curved heart line indicates the equally unhealthy opposite: too great a willingness to concede, to the point of modifying one's own personality.

The heart line should be read from the Jupiter end. Its proximity to the fingers indicates the degree to which the head rules the heart; if it's close, the head rules to a great degree, and vice versa.

Lots of small branches outward from the heart line show receptivity to new people.

A heart line starting high on Jupiter indicates that the chosen partner should be someone to look up to. Should it travel across the hand to Upper Mars, work is probably very important and may supersede affairs of the heart.

A person with a short heart line, hugging the fingers and directed straight at Saturn, is practical in matters of love and may be promiscuous without suffering a bad conscience or a broken heart.

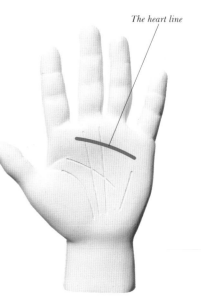

The heart line

The Simian line is unusual. It is only one line, the head and heart line combined; it usually belongs to a person who is dangerously intense and jealous, and finds it difficult to control their emotions.

THE FATE LINE

Not only are the three vertical lines on the hand usually harder to distinguish than the three main horizontal lines, but they sometimes fail to appear at all. If there is no fate line (roughly from the wrist up to Saturn), the subject will have to find their own way in life without a great deal of cultural, emotional, or financial capital from their family. However, sometimes this line appears later, starting not at the wrist, but up near the head line or the Plain of Mars (the center of the hand).

The fate line is sometimes called the line of Saturn. It represents the central supporting practical aspect of one's being, that may include career, marriage, or children. A fate line that begins inside the mound of Venus can mean family interference in one's personal ambition or romantic life. The fate line beginning at the head line shows the person has achieved much through academic effort. However, a previously good line suddenly stopping at the heart line, usually means some kind of sexual indiscretion.

Any undue thickness or deepness shows that there is a period of anxiety at that time in life (chronological time being read from the wrist end).

_The fate line

THE FATE LINE INDICATES THE EFFECT THAT OUTSIDE INFLUENCES HAVE UPON OUR DESTINY.

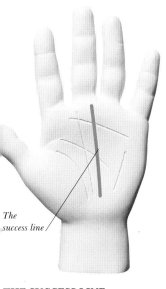

The success line

Its direction, and the location of its commencement, can be an indication of progress, but it is not unusual for successful individuals to have a broken Apollo line, if indeed, one at all.

THE HEALTH LINE

The health line (also called the Mercury line) ends toward the little finger, and usually runs from Venus or the radial side. It may

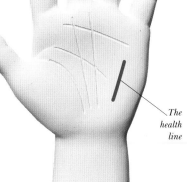

The health line

THE SUCCESS LINE

The success line, or line of Apollo, should, like other vertical lines, be thin and unwavering. This is the line of fame and fortune, but also of success in whatever field the individual finds important. The line may start on the palm or higher; a break in it indicates a period of struggle. If it is altogether absent, the person is not a fatalist. They do not trust luck or chance, but believe that they must work hard to achieve what they want.

indicate baseless hypochondria or preoccupation with health. A crossed, weak line signifies an ongoing health problem. A health line that begins at Venus, near the thumb, may mean poor digestion; on a very lined hand, a long health line reveals a danger of ulcers from worry. Ideally, a health line should not be visible at all.

The rare line, or crescent, of intuition is not to be confused with the health line. It curves around Upper Mars, from Luna to Mercury, and indicates an intuitive person, even a psychic.

THE FATE LINE CAN DETERMINE CAREER, LIFESTYLE, AND FAMILY.

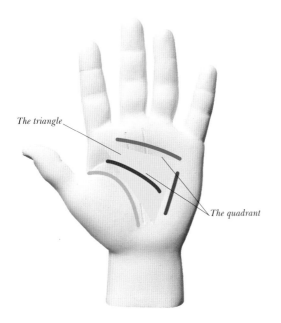

The triangle

The quadrant

THE TRIANGLE
AND QUADRANT

The great triangle is formed by the three main lines of head, heart, and life, plus the health line – that may cross to the life line forming a triangle, but, equally, may not. A wide triangle indicates openness, a quick arousal of the passions, and a willingness to take action. If it is small and cramped, it shows pettiness of spirit.

The quadrant is the area between the heart and head lines in which the palmist reads impulsiveness, self-control, and the capacity to confront convention. If this area is very wide, the person is a creature of impulse and pays very little attention to what anyone else thinks. If, on the other hand, it is small and criss-crossed with a network of lines, this is a troubled, frightened, and timid person, who is overconcerned about other people's opinions.

THOSE WHO ENJOY THE BEST HEALTH
ARE LIKELY TO HAVE NO HEALTH LINE.

PLOTTING DATES
ON THE LINES

To plot a life's chronology along the lines, to assess whether events have already happened or when they may do, one must know where the lines begin. Always read the horizontal lines from the radial (thumb) side, and the vertical ones from the wrist. Be flexible when gauging time; think of the palmprint as a clock with age fifty situated at a quarter to the hour on the life line. Life partners may see life events recorded at similar times along their life lines.

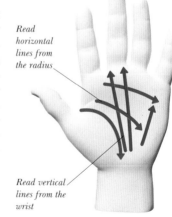

Read horizontal lines from the radius

Read vertical lines from the wrist

THE STAR

The star is a sign of some spectacular occurrence, although not always good – whether it signifies a lottery win or a broken leg depends on other things. For instance, a star on the mound of Jupiter means great achievement if it is on the right hand, whereas if the star is on the left, it merely means a sudden stroke of fortune. This distinction applies, of course, to all readings: the left hand shows potential, the right, actual.

We shall, however, assume that the star is always something you wish to see, in which case a star on Saturn means a leap in knowledge; on Apollo, artistic triumph; on Mercury, dramatic success in business or public life. On Venus, it may mean a happy love affair; on Luna, success in writing. However, a star terminating the head, life, or heart lines, predicts a sudden upset of the part that is indicated by the particular line.

A VIOLINIST'S HANDS ARE VITAL TO HER SKILL — AND HOLD SIGNS OF HER MUSICAL EXCELLENCE.

THE DOT AND THE TRIDENT

Dots are not usually good signs, as they tend to appear where there is illness or crisis.

The trident is always an excellent sign, as it signifies lasting happiness rather than sudden surprising acclaim or good fortune. Thus a heart or head line that ends in a trident is a predictor of fulfillment in love, or through the application of intelligence, respectively.

ISLANDS

 Islands, uneven circles on lines or mounds, mean change that may be unwelcome, but may lead to better things later on. An island represents a division in energies, later re-united.

On the line of Apollo, an island can signify a storm, or perhaps some scandal. On the life line, islands near the start mean a troubled youth; islands at the very start indicate some mystery surrounding the person's birth, perhaps illegitimacy. Islands, or even short lines, connecting the start of the life line to the head line, suggest that the person was looked after in her youth by people who were not blood relations.

LINES AND CROSSES

 Crosses, grilles, and lines tend to draw out the negative aspect of the mound or line they are found upon. They signify bad luck, dashed hopes, and troubles, although the palmist must view these marks together with the overall formation of the hand and not in isolation. Thus, a grille found on Venus may indicate greedy lust, rather than desire; a cross found on

Venus may mean a tendency to duplicity in love.

Wherever they are found, these markings are indicators of confusion or obsession, lack of control or fading will. Small horizontal lines on the ulna, the outer edge of the palm away from the thumb, are an indication of travel.

Elsewhere on the hand, bold vertical lines are generally negative in whatever sphere they are found. However a branch up from a line is a good sign, but a branch down is more dubious.

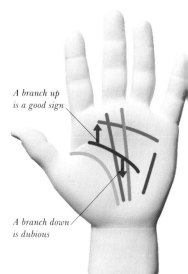

A branch up is a good sign

A branch down is dubious

A CAMERAMAN'S CREATIVITY IS AN
EXAMPLE OF THE POSITIVE EFFECT
OF AN ISOLATED TRIANGLE.

THE SQUARE
AND THE TRIANGLE

The square is a protective marking. A square on a mound neutralizes any problems revealed on that mound, and a square around a poor omen, such as an island, protects against the omen's effects. However, in its unhappy aspect, the square may show confinement or even imprisonment. For instance, a square on Venus reveals that the person has been held back in some way by their family.

An isolated triangle brings out the positive aspect of whatever mound it is found on. On Venus, it indicates contentment in the affections; on Luna, creativity, particularly in writing or film-making.

MAIN MOUNDS

Mounds – the pads or bumps around the palm – may be flat or even hollow. Judge the relative importance of each mound in conjunction with the length of the fingers, the lines, and anything else of note.

THE MOUND OF MERCURY

 Mercury, the mound or pad below the little finger, is the mound of self-expression, travel, and business acumen.

A person who has pointed fingers and a noticeable mound of Mercury will usually be a good public speaker. If they have square fingers, they will be more inclined to take part in dogged argument and debate.

Where the mound of Mercury is hollow and unlined, the person concerned is likely to be shy, perhaps even lazy, while deep lines on the mound of Mercury may be indicative of garrulousness.

Mercury is the shrewd, active god of merchants, but also the god of thieves.

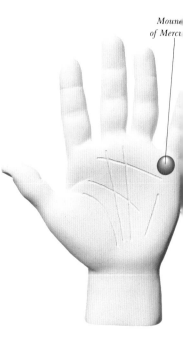

Mound
of Mercu

THE MOUND OF APOLLO

Apollo, the mound or pad below the fourth finger, is the warm, masculine, sun sign; it represents charm, creativity, and success. The possessor of a strong Apollo mound may be a high-achieving sports-person or actor. On the other hand they could, if Apollo is not kept in check, be a gambler who is indiscriminate in their personal friendships. Apollo undeveloped indicates a person who fails to appreciate spectacle, color, and ceremony.

The opposite of Apollo is Luna, the chaste, cool, feminine sign of the Moon. A woman wears a ring on her left Apollo finger to show the link between sun and moon.

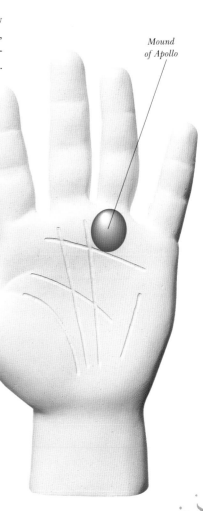

Mound of Apollo

41

THE MOUND OF SATURN

Saturn overdeveloped may imply someone who is so intent on keeping their nose to the ground that they never have time to view their surroundings (or even notice what their partner is doing). They are busy earning money, or otherwise thinking about the practical side of life. If their Saturn mound is not counterbalanced by other symbols in the hand, they may be overserious. More positively, they may be a prudent, sober person whose caution serves them well.

Mound of Saturn

THE MOUND OF VENUS

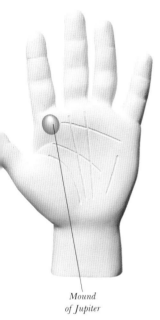

Venus, below the thumb, is the mound of all that is harmonious and loving. Far more than sex, it includes love of life, family, all that is sensual, and musical harmony. It should be firm and smooth in the hand. A depression covering Venus is a sign of indolence, carelessness, and generally flaccid attitudes. Horizontal lines show interference by one's family, but vertical lines mean efforts have been made to rebuild family relationships.

Mound of Jupiter

THE MOUND OF JUPITER

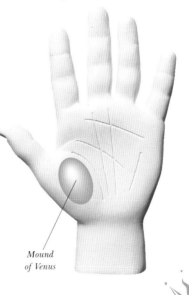

Jupiter represents the practical use of will-power, ambition, and executive strength. It shows a capacity to put beliefs – perhaps religious – into practice. The possessor of a well-developed Jupiter likes order and discipline, but can be arrogant. Should Jupiter be underdeveloped, they tend to dislike authority and lack ambition.

Mound of Venus

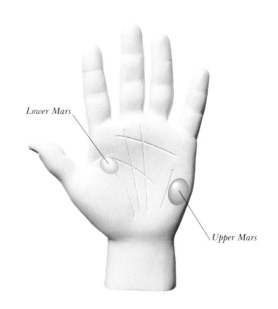

Lower Mars

Upper Mars

UPPER AND LOWER MARS

A well-developed Upper Mars, located on the ulna side of the hand, shows adequate aggression in life; the person will be able to stick up for themselves in difficult situations, but will also be tenacious in everything they begin. Any overdevelopment in this area means a tendency to violence or stubbornness, while underdevelopment means timidity; this person does not possess an assertive nature and will be put off far too easily.

Lower Mars, which is found on the radial side of the hand, represents motivation, and the ability to get things moving. Small vertical lines are a good sign in this area as they indicate discretion.

THE PLAIN OF MARS
AND THE LUNAR MOUND

Mars rules the parts of the hand
that the moon and sun don't,
including the Plain of Mars,
or the hollow in the middle of
the palm. Distinct, unbroken
lines around it show health,
prosperity, and a long life. It
should be flat, for optimism, as
a hollow Plain of Mars indicates
lack of confidence and drive.

The Lunar mound, situated
to the ulna side of the Plain of
Mars and below Upper Mars, is
related to
the uncon-
scious and to
travel. Depending
on its juxtaposition
with the head line, this
mound can signify great
inspiration, or it can mean
a tendency to lie. It may be
seen to grow and diminish, like
the moon, according to the over-
whelmingly positive or negative
attitudes of the subject.

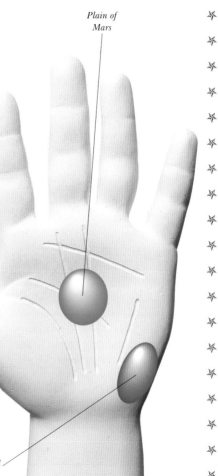

Plain of Mars

Lunar mound

PREDICTION

Most of what you predict about your subject's future you will have learned, not from seeing future events marked in the hand, but from a reading of their character. Although certain signs indicate change, whether that is good or bad is something you can know only by understanding their personality and reaction.

A SUMMARY OF FORTUNATE SIGNS

 Some signs are so positive that their influence will override most misfortunes. So, if you see a very good sign in a life that seems prone to adversity, don't be surprised.

Understand the kind of person you are dealing with, and how they will react. Many previously ordinary people discover, in a crisis, reserves of courage they never knew they had. Some are immeasurably strengthened by a disaster that would defeat most of us.

- ❻ *A trident at the top of the fate line is a very good sign, as is a trident at the end of the life line or at the start of the heart line.*
- ❻ *A line inside the line of life on both hands indicates inherited wealth.*
- ❻ *Long lines leading upward from the line of life indicate success.*

The nature of that success can be predicted according to the mound of the line's destination.
- ❻ *A line away from the life line to Luna may indicate emigration.*
- ❻ *A line from the wrist to Apollo indicates that a person will enjoy a full and happy life.*

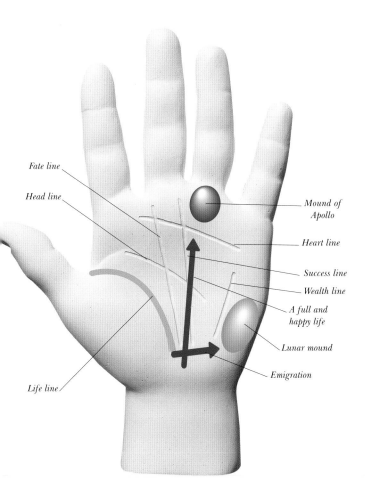

Fate line

Head line

Mound of
Apollo

Heart line

Success line

Wealth line

A full and
happy life

Lunar mound

Emigration

Life line

HEALTH, WEALTH, OR HAPPINESS —
SOME GOOD SIGNS ARE STRONG
ENOUGH TO OUTWEIGH BAD ONES.

HEALTH WARNINGS AND RINGS

Our fingernails and hands change according to our state of health. Rings also change the markings of our hands, and have their own meanings, according to the type and size, and the fingers upon which they are worn. Observation will often reveal that a finger is "waisted," perhaps because a ring has been worn for many years but has been removed for some reason, leaving a mark

HEART, HEAD, AND LIFE LINES, AND OTHER SIGNS,
CAN WARN US OF HEALTH AND FITNESS PROBLEMS.

Cheese is a good source of protein

Bread provides essential fiber

Pasta provides energy

Vegetables are a useful source of vitamins and minerals

A HEALTHY DIET WILL BE REFLECTED IN A
MORE POSITIVE PALM READING.

HEALTH WARNINGS

The three lines of heart, head, and life on the dominant hand represent the physical organs of the body, with the life line relating to stomach and liver. The palmist's skill lies in noticing signs in relation to each other.

If the hand is clenched, with the thumb held inside, one may infer extreme tension, and must watch for signs of ulcers or heart trouble. A twisted Apollo finger is similarly indicative of emotional repression and confusion that will affect the body. Should Mercury be deficient, watch out for diseases of the bladder and kidneys.

Tassels and feathering toward the end of the life line are warning signs of a potential health weakness. This can be pre-empted in good time if the person switches to a healthy and wholesome diet, takes plenty of exercise, and learns to find the time for proper relaxation.

Low moons on the fingernails, or horizontal ridges, could indicate a recent episode of poor health, but you should remember that fingernails take six months to grow fully, so it is possible that such signs may be long out of date. If, when seen from the side, the nails appear to be concave, it may mean that the person is suffering from poor circulation.

RINGS

Try, when you look at rings as a palmist, to ignore fashion.

In general, big rings are worn by attention-seekers, and what matters most is the finger to which attention is unconsciously being drawn. A ring worn on a short Jupiter of the minor hand, for instance, reveals unresolved inner problems. These may already be showing themselves in dysfunctional or self-destructive behavior of some kind. Yet a ring on a short Jupiter of the dominant hand denotes a desire to control other people. On a long Jupiter of the minor hand, there is self-deprecation or even guilt; on a long Jupiter of the domi-nant hand, a ring means a tendency to blame others for everything that goes wrong.

A very large ring, or many rings, on the wedding finger draws attention to difficulties with one's marriage; Princess Diana wore a spectacular ring the day after her divorce.

Rings on little fingers, particularly of the minor hand, indicate sexual ambiva-lence, either repressed homosexuality or some other inner duality which is prob-ably so sublimated as to be invisible on the dominant hand. A ring on the thumb, traditionally the Venusian, phallic digit, is a sign that potency is of much concern to the wearer.

LARGE RINGS OFTEN INDICATE ATTTENTION-SEEKING, AND MAY REVEAL UNSOLVED MARITAL PROBLEMS.

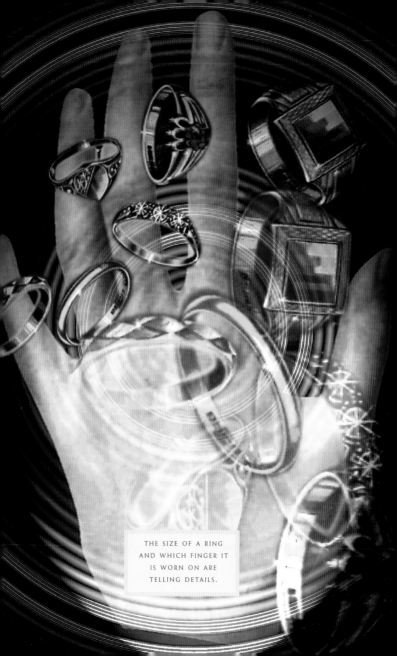

THE SIZE OF A RING
AND WHICH FINGER IT
IS WORN ON ARE
TELLING DETAILS.

A PALMISTRY CHART

SUBJECT

- 🌀 *Male aged 28*
- 🌀 *Hand classification: square*
- 🌀 *Thumb: long*
- 🌀 *Fingers: short*
- 🌀 *Fingernails: rounded, short but wide*

- 🌀 *Fingertips: conic but note spatulate Apollo, particularly on the left hand*
- 🌀 *Knuckles: not pronounced*
- 🌀 *Skin: warm, fleshy, firm*
- 🌀 *Mounds: notable Mound of Jupiter on right hand*

REMARKS

 The overwhelming impression is of a healthy, self-reliant person without any hangups. All the markings point to someone who will achieve through dogged persistence.

The high mound of Jupiter indicates ambition and dynamism in someone with a strong will – this impression is supported by the long thumb, notably long for such a classically square hand.

There is one acute difference between the right and left hands. On the left, Apollo is weak and spatulate, indicating a dependent, more emotional, but less imaginative person prone to panic. Apollo and Saturn are set close together, indicating conflict between strong emotions and the need to get on with life. The right hand is Saturnian and controlled. Because this tempers the weakness in Apollo on the right, and because impetus is so strong, it is safe to assume that this person has learned to "pull himself together" by an effort of will.

Mercury leans away from Apollo; at times of stress this person withdraws from other people, re-orders his life and gets on with the long task of self-help.

LEFT HAND

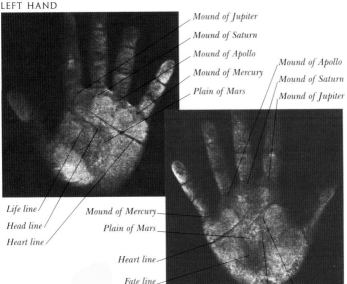

Mound of Jupiter

Mound of Saturn

Mound of Apollo

Mound of Mercury

Plain of Mars

Mound of Apollo

Mound of Saturn

Mound of Jupiter

Life line

Head line

Heart line

Mound of Mercury

Plain of Mars

Heart line

Fate line

RIGHT HAND   Life line   Head line

The wide, round fingernails indicate a placid temperament and the flat plain of Mars, optimism.

The life line, rather chaotically joined to the head line at the start and even running double for a while, shows there has been some turmoil or uncertainty at the start of life. However upward branches towards Apollo on the head line, once the confusion is sorted out, indicate a turning toward the arts.

The heart line shows a long lasting deep relationship and some close connection with artistic work. Maybe, as the heart line persists to Upper Mars, this person will work closely with his partner for many years.

The fate line is especially marked on the right hand, and shows strong family support throughout his life. A triangle near the start of the line shows that there was a period of great tranquility and happiness in childhood.

✦

CONCLUSION

✦

You should now be equipped with a basic knowledge of palmistry, and an understanding as to how the finer details of the hands are linked with personal characteristics and destiny. You must remember, however, that even though many palmists have made amazingly accurate prophecies of future events, you should regard palmistry as a useful and enjoyable tool, that allows you or your subject to understand life's ups and downs. Use what you see in the readings as a guide, be it to help curb a reckless streak, or even unleash a creative potential. As is the case with all arts of prediction, remind yourself that forewarned is forearmed!

A VERY IMPORTANT POSTSCRIPT

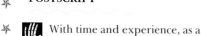 With time and experience, as a palm-reader you will grow increasingly sensitive to the moods of the people who come to see you. It will be apparent that while some see palm-reading as a harmless diversion, and others are introspective but strong and forward-looking, there are a few who, for whatever reason, are at a vulnerable point in their lives. Try to take special care of their feelings, and never communicate despondency or depression. People should leave a palmist feeling hopeful and positive about their lives.

Finally, and perhaps most importantly, your subject should feel assured that what has passed between the two of you during the reading will remain entirely confidential. You must never gossip to others about those who come to you for a reading.

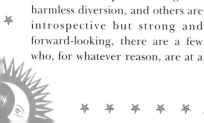

FURTHER READING

ALTMAN, N. *Discover Palmistry*, (Aquarian, Wellingborough, 1991)

BASHIR, MIR, *The Art of Hand Analysis*, (Muller, London, 1981)

BROEKMAN, M., *The Complete Encyclopedia of Practical Palmistry*, (Chancellor, London, 1975)

CHEIRO, *Cheiro's Guide to the Hand*, (Barne & Jenkins, London, 1975)

DAS, S. K., *Everybody's Guide to Palmistry*, (Oriental University, London, 1986)

DAY, S. B. AND STACEY, B, *A Hindu Interpretation of the Hand*, (University of Minneapolis Medical School, 1973)

KWOK MAN HO, *Lines of Destiny*, (Rider, London, 1986)

REID, LORI, *The Female Hand*, (Aquarian, Wellingborough, 1986)

WARREN-DAVIS, DYLAN, *The Hand Reveals*, (Element, Shaftesbury, 1993)

THE PALMIST, BATHELEMY COCLES TAKEN FROM HIS EARLY 16TH CENTURY BOOK ON CHROMANCY

THE 17TH-CENTURY PAINTER DAVID TENNIERS AND HIS WIFE CONSULT A PALMIST

INDEX